New Seasons is a registered trademark of Publications International, Ltd.

© 2015 New Seasons
All rights reserved.
This publication may not be reproduced in whole or in part by any means
whatsoever without written permission from:

Louis Weber, CEO
Publications International, Ltd.
7373 North Cicero Avenue
Lincolnwood, Illinois 60712

www.pilbooks.com

Permission is never granted for commercial purposes.

Manufactured in China.

8 7 6 5 4 3 2 1

ISBN: 978-1-68022-159-6

Laugh Lines
Getting Old Is Funny!

Written by Alison Pohn

new seasons®

Stanley, I think they've changed to smaller stools since we were last here.

Ed's smile turned to a frown when he realized his wife had said "steaks," not "shakes," for dinner.

Here's a tip:

Cabana suit on.

Chin up.

Earl could never figure out why Lena was always so refreshed after an afternoon of errands in town.

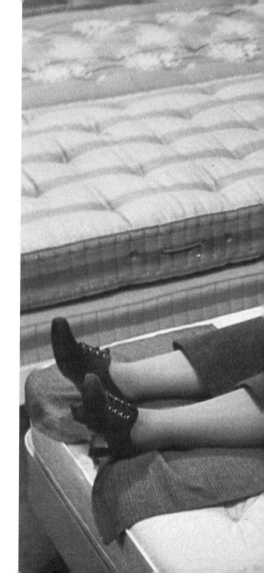

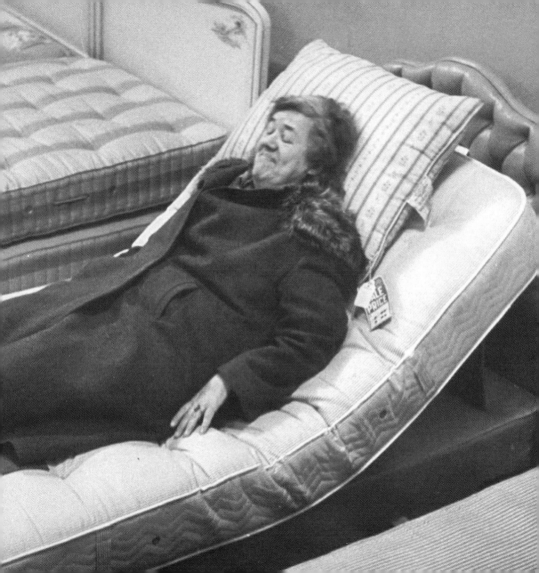

Sure, it wasn't the Chippendales,
but the women of Shady Springs
Retirement Home appreciated the effort.

Mary-Kate and Ashley,

consider this a warning.

13

Myra decided to revisit the issue of hormone replacement therapy.

Oh, sure. You're

fooling everyone.

By her 13th grandchild,

Ida had become pretty laid-back.

Men. Who needs 'em?

Being beautiful is hard work.

—Eleanor, how did you get

those shapely thighs?

—Why, walking 10 miles

to and from school,

uphill both ways,

you silly girl.

I've got those falling down arches,

can't see without my glasses,

I hate gravity blues.

Oh, great. This means my husband's at home walking a fried chicken.

Don't get excited.
I'm only checking
my balance.

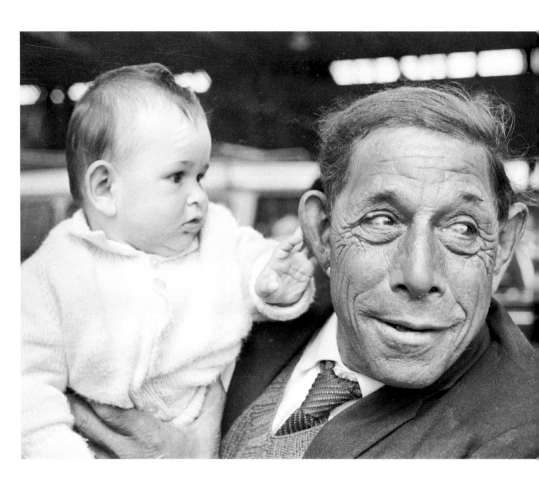

I think Grandpa has a squirrel in his ear!

"Be good and you

will be lonesome."

—Mark Twain

Careful, Marshall, or you'll end up
with both sets of teeth.

My body's a temple—the temple of doom.

The girls liked to park it right outside Starbucks and taunt the clients with real, percolated coffee.

Remember when your daily workout was more than just tying your shoes?

Margie remembered—albeit too late—
where she'd put the leftover rice pudding.

Helen slept on,

secure in the knowledge that

no one else on the bus

remembered where they

were going either.

Cute babe.

Awesome blue rinse.

Don't look. Okay, quick, look!

Fifty-two Christmases,

fifty-two house dresses.

Are you sure this is

the fountain of youth?

Take the picture already.
We're wrinkling like
prunes in here.

Don't mind me.
I'm just sitting here
working out my
retirement plan.

It's nothing fancy—

just my address.

Kings of the

Wild Frontier, indeed.

Oh, no dear. We don't want to buy insurance. We just wanted some company.

Stayin' alive!

Stayin' alive!

Beauty really is skin deep.

This one . . .

This one's about the

size of my prostate.

Why, I believe this gum

is older than we are!

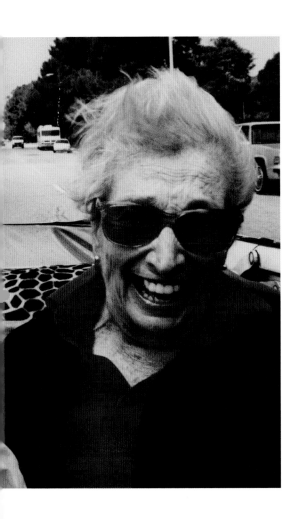

Girls still wanna

have fun.

Photography credits:

Front and Back Cover: © Roy Morsch/CORBIS
© Leland Bobbé/CORBIS; © Brand X Pictures; © CORBIS; © Mark
Downey/Index Stock Imagery; © Natalie Fobes/CORBIS; © Ewing
Galloway/Index Stock Imagery; © Getty Images: Hulton Archive, Hulton
Archive/Evening Standard, Hulton Archive/McCabe, Hulton Archive/John
Pratt, Hulton Archive/Wood, Stone/Erik Dreyer, Stone/Michael Edwards,
Time Life Pictures, Time Life Pictures/Ed Clark, Time Life Pictures/John
Dominis, Time Life Pictures/Mark Kauffman, Time Life Pictures/Leonard
McCombe, Time Life Pictures/Francis Miller, Time Life Pictures/George
Silk; © Philip Gould/CORBIS; © Cat Gwynn/CORBIS; © Hulton-
Deutsch Collection/CORBIS; © Ken Kaminesky/CORBIS; © Helen
King/CORBIS; © Ray Morsch/CORBIS; © Cynthia Diane Pringle/
CORBIS; © Anthony Redpath/CORBIS; © Trinette Reed/CORBIS;
© Howard Sokol/Index Stock Imagery; © Strauss/Curtis/CORBIS;
© Michael S. Yamashita/CORBIS